# THE WOMAN AT THE WELL

## Stephanie M Seaton

**Self Published through KDP Publishing**

# DEDICATION

This book is dedicated to the broken little girl that was trapped inside me. The little girl no one saw. The little girl who didn't get to live as a little girl. The little girl that I continually cried for until I finally told her story. This is for you, "Tanky," "Steph" and some called her "Steph Marie."

# Table of Contents

# PREFACE

John 4
New International Version
Jesus Talks with a Samaritan Woman

Now Jesus learned that the Pharisees had heard that he was gaining and baptizing more disciples than John — Although, in fact, it was not Jesus who baptized, but his disciples. So he left Judea and went back once more to Galilee. Now, he had to go through Samaria. So he came to a town in Samaria called Sychar, near the plot of ground Jacob had given to his son Joseph. Jacob's well was there, and Jesus, tired as he was from the journey, sat down by the well. It was about noon. When a Samaritan woman came to draw water, Jesus said to her, "Will you give me a drink?" (His disciples had gone into the town to buy food.)

The Samaritan woman said to him, "You are a Jew, and I am a Samaritan woman. How can you ask me for a drink?" (For Jews do not associate with Samaritans.[a]) Jesus answered her, "If you knew the gift of God and who it is that asks you for a drink, you would have asked him, and he would have given you living water."
"Sir," the woman said, "you have nothing to draw with, and the well is deep. Where can you get this living water? Are you greater than our father Jacob, who gave us the

well and drank from it himself, as did also his sons and his livestock?"

Jesus answered, "Everyone who drinks this water will be thirsty again, but whoever drinks the water I give them will never thirst. Indeed, the water I give them will become in them a spring of water welling up to eternal life."
The woman said to him, "Sir, give me this water so that I won't get thirsty and have to keep coming here to draw water."
He told her, "Go, call your husband and come back."
"I have no husband," she replied.

Jesus said to her, "You are right when you say you have no husband. The fact is, you have had five husbands, and the man you now have is not your husband. What you have just said is quite true."
"Sir," the woman said, "I can see that you are a prophet. Our ancestors worshiped on this mountain, but you Jews claim that the place where we must worship is in Jerusalem."

"Woman," Jesus replied, "believe me, a time is coming when you will worship the Father neither on this mountain nor in Jerusalem. You Samaritans worship what you do not know; we worship what we do know, for salvation is from the Jews. Yet a time is coming and has now come when the true worshipers will worship the Father in the Spirit and in truth, for they are the kind of worshipers the Father seeks. God is spirit, and his worshipers must worship in the Spirit and in truth."
The woman said, "I know that Messiah (called Christ) "is

coming. When he comes, he will explain everything to us."

Then Jesus declared, "I, the one speaking to you—I am he.

## The Disciples Rejoin Jesus

Just then, his disciples returned and were surprised to find him talking with a woman. But no one asked, "What do you want?" or "Why are you talking with her?" Then, leaving her water jar, the woman went back to the town and said to the people, "Come, see a man who told me everything I ever did. Could this be the Messiah?"

They came out of the town and made their way toward him. Meanwhile, his disciples urged him, "Rabbi, eat something." But he said to them, "I have food to eat that you know nothing about." Then his disciples said to each other, "Could someone have brought him food?"

"My food," said Jesus, "is to do the will of him who sent me and to finish his work.

Don't you have a saying, 'It's still four months until harvest'? I tell you, open your eyes and look at the fields! They are ripe for harvest. Even now, the one who reaps draws a wage and harvests a crop for eternal life so that the sower and the reaper may be glad together. Thus, the saying 'One sows and another reaps' is true. I sent you to reap what you have not worked for. Others have done the hard work, and you have reaped the benefits of their labor."

## Many Samaritans Believe

Many of the Samaritans from that town believed in him because of the woman's testimony,
"He told me everything I ever did." So when the Samaritans came to him, they urged him to stay with them, and he stayed two days. And because of his words, many more became believers.
They said to the woman, "We no longer believe just because of what you said; now we have heard for ourselves, and we know that this man really is the Savior of the world."
"The Woman At The Well"

I can identify with the woman at the well. I have been a broken woman. I have been on the run from my true self. I have had several distractions from tall, dark handsomes. Some were not so tall, lol.
When you hear the story of the Woman at the Well, we don't get to hear what her life journey was that brought her to that place of desperation.

We hear her sin as a label.

We just know she was thirsty for love for sure. We gather this from multiple husbands.
What touches my heart is that she went through life being judged by her choices to find love and acceptance.

Yet, the reality is that no one in her life had actually taken the time to show her the love she longed so badly for.

That was my story as well.

I finally reached desperation after a third failed marriage

and asked Jesus to personally show me love and father me. I wanted to feel loved, wanted and needed.

Then my healing journey began.

The story of the woman at the well demonstrates that Jesus comes to the least of us. He meets us right where we are. He cares for the outcasts. The people that are judged. The Samaritan woman was considered low because of her sex, ethnicity, and relationship history, but none of that mattered to Jesus because he saw her need for love and salvation.

In our weakest and most vulnerable moments is when we SEE him the most.

The Samaritan woman even despised herself. She was tired of herself and her repeated cycles. Jesus recognised her spiritual thirst and engaged with her. This was a designated encounter.

Verse 4 is a digression to explain God's purpose for Jesus going through Samaria. 4 But. The "but" here indicates a qualification.

This may indicate that there was a divine purpose in Jesus' taking an unusual route to Galilee from Judea. It was God's will that Jesus meet the woman at the well.
He was waiting for her. Just like he still waits for us. When he comes, he will explain everything to us." Jesus then reveals himself to the Samaritan woman.

"I, the one speaking to you — I am he." Meaning he is everything she ever needed.

The grace of God is always there for everyone. Regardless of the entanglements, distractions and drama of our lives, He loves all of us enough to actively keep seeking us, to draw us to His intimacy and into relationship with him.

There came a woman from Samaria to draw water. Jesus said to her, "Give me a drink." For his disciples had gone away into the city to buy food. The Samaritan woman said to him, "How is it that you, a Jew, ask for a drink from me, a woman of Samaria?" For Jews have no dealings with Samaritans.

John 4:10 Jesus answered and said unto her, if thou knewest the gift of God, and who it is that saith to thee, give me to drink; thou wouldest have asked of him, and he would have given thee living water.

This is what fills the THIRST in our hearts. She would no longer be:

The Husband Stealer

The woman with too much baggage

The five time divorcee

Nor any other label society had attached to her.

This story will compare the life of the character Sheila's life experiences to the imagined experiences of The woman at the well.

This book is based on a few factual experiences and several created experiences to bring the story of the Woman at the Well to full sight.

# FOREWORD

God has allowed me to see life from a number
of vantage points. From the public
school hallways to the sacred walls of the
church. We are all the picture of God's
grace and mercy. God's miraculous work
does not discriminate. People of all
backgrounds, ethnicities, and ages can
experience His power. I can testify that
once you have an encounter with God then your life
will never be the same.While God was shaping the
lives of others.I learned that he was also strategically
building something more in me.This was not apparent
on the onset.but life has a way of showing you a lesson
that you will later use in life. In other words,the person
you are becoming is a direct reflection of what God
has brought you through.The words of the old hymn
ring true,"We will understand it better By and By!"

God has a way of showing us just how much He care
by sending partners that have a heart for ministry.
Stephanie Seaton is more than my Sister in Christ, she
has become a partner in this Kingdom Building
work. I have watched her grow in
her relationship with Christ, as well as grow in
the calling that God has on her life.If we are not
growing then we are stagnate.My God is a progressive

God,which means we have no place for stagnation.This
only leaves growing in God as the only option .
As a part of growth in God comes the maturation
of our faith and understanding
that God uses the sum total of our circumstances
for His glory. Seaton hasfiction. This masterful work
will bring you to the conclusion that regardless of
your past, that our God sees, He knows, and
He still cares. His transformative love
covers my darkest moments.

Let's take this journey and remember that God will
take the good, bad and indifferent and use it
for our benefit as well as for His glory.

Rev. Rodney C. Curry

# CHAPTER 1

# **Basic Needs**

We are not privileged to the details of the childhood of the woman at the well. However, we do know that there are some basic needs for every child.

When a child's basic needs are not met, it can have serious consequences for their physical, emotional, and cognitive development. The most fundamental needs that must be met for a child to thrive include nutritious food, adequate rest, a safe and stable environment, and access to medical care when necessary.

When a child does not have enough to eat or lacks access to healthy food choices, their physical health can suffer. Malnutrition can lead to stunted growth, weakened immune systems, and other health problems. Similarly, when a child does not get enough sleep or lives in an unstable or unsafe environment, it can impact their emotional wellbeing and cognitive development.

If a child's basic needs are not being met, it is important to identify and address the underlying issues as soon as possible. This may involve working with social services or other organizations to provide the necessary resources and support to the child and their family.

Ultimately, ensuring that every child has their basic needs met is essential for their health, happiness, and future success.

An unhappy childhood can have a lasting impact on a person's life. Childhood experiences can shape our personalities, our relationships, and our overall outlook on life. Growing up in an environment that is emotionally or physically abusive, neglectful, or unstable can lead to a variety of negative outcomes.

Children who experience trauma or stress at a young age may struggle with anxiety, depression, and other mental health issues as adults. In addition, they may have difficulty forming healthy relationships, trusting others, and regulating their emotions.

However, it's important to note that not everyone who experiences a difficult childhood will have negative outcomes. Many individuals are able to overcome their past and thrive in their adult lives. Seeking support from friends, family, or a mental health professional can be a crucial first step in healing from the effects of an unhappy childhood.

Sheila, our main character, did not receive the basic needs of a human in her childhood. The lack of these basic needs in Sheila and "The Woman At The Well" are a direct reason for the traumatic lives they both experienced.

Glory be to our Lord, who always triumphs.

A child's basic needs include:

Security
Kids must feel safe and sound, with their basic survival needs met: shelter, food, clothing, medical care and protection from harm.

Stability. Stability comes from family and community.

Consistency

Emotional support
Love

Education

Positive role models

Structure

Children need to know that your love does not depend on his or her accomplishments. All children need their basic needs met in order to thrive throughout childhood and adulthood. There should be grace for mistakes, and/or defeats should be expected and accepted. Confidence grows in a home that is full of unconditional love and affection.

When children do not have affectionate parents, they tend to have lower self-esteem and to feel more lonely, hostile, aggressive, and depressed. It causes you to seek that love and affection in all the wrong people and places.

Who lets a four-year-old little girl walk to the store with a grown cousin who has to be in his twenties. Not even a first cousin. He was probably a second or third that

Sheila doesn't even know.

All those trips to the store never ended up going straight to the store. It ended with pit stops behind the store where he would open her clothes and begin to fondle her and touch her inappropriately, making her feel dirty and nasty.

Then he would say those words which made Sheila feel even worse "pretty little girl". She hated to hear the words pretty little girl.

That was Sheila's first experience of being sexually abused.This was not a one time occurance.The sad thing is no adult recognized this was a bad choice.

Abuse is a serious issue that affects many people worldwide. It can take many different forms, including physical, emotional, sexual, and financial abuse. Regardless of the type of abuse, it can have long-term effects on the victim's mental and physical health.

Especially when they feel forced to "keep the secret " or they are threatened with further consequences for telling someone.This sounds like part of "The Woman At The Wells" diagnosis.

One of the most important things to remember is that abuse is never the victim's fault. No matter what the abuser says or does, the victim is not to blame. It can be difficult for victims to come forward and seek help, but it is important for them to know that there are resources available to them.

If you or someone you know is experiencing abuse, there

are many organizations and hotlines that can provide support and assistance. It is important to reach out for help and to know that you are not alone. Remember that abuse is a serious issue, but there is hope for recovery and healing.

Sheila's parents were married, but you could always tell they weren't happy. Her earliest memories of her parents together was her dad leaving on Friday, not returning home until Monday after work. He was living his best life,according to her mother.

He was supposedly wasting the families money on liquor and women.He was also sharing parts of himself that only his wife should have known. This led to her mother being stressed and frustrated quite often.

Who do you think felt the weight of that stress and frustration?

Her mother was feeling desperation.She started verbally abusing Sheila at an early age. Verbal abuse towards a child can cause lasting emotional damage, and it is important to understand the impact it can have. Verbal abuse can come in many forms, from name-calling to yelling or screaming at a child. It can also include any language that belittles or humiliates a child, or that makes them feel worthless or unloved.

Children who experience verbal abuse may suffer from low self-esteem, depression, anxiety, and even post-traumatic stress disorder. They may also struggle with forming healthy relationships and trusting others.This sounds like part of "The Woman At The Wells" diagnosis.

It is crucial for adults to be aware of the language they use when communicating with children and to avoid any form of verbal abuse.

Instead, adults should aim to communicate with children in a positive and constructive manner, providing them with support and encouragement to build their self-confidence and emotional well-being. If you suspect that a child is experiencing verbal abuse, it is important to seek professional help immediately.

Sheila should never have been made to feel that she deserved to bear the weight of her mothers frustrations. Sheila was made responsible for her younger sibling at an early age.
One day, they were driving down the street, and she was holding her baby brother in her little arms.

Suddenly, the sun was reflecting in her brother's face, the mother screamed and shouted at Sheila to pull down the sun visor to block the sun. Her mother screamed every day. It was the regular tone for communication.
Her mother moved in with her grandparents after the divorce. She now found herself living in a house with her aunts, uncles and grandparents. It was absolute dysfunction. There were 10 to 12 people sharing one small frame, three bedroom, two bath house.

Sharing a small house with 10 people was very challenging. There was no clear communication, organization, nor respect. Everyone was not on the same page and did not agree to follow any set rules.Established boundaries were never set.There was no such thing as having your own personal space.

Arguing was the normal style of communication to address conflicts.There was not a good standard of housekeeping in place. No one cleaned up after themselves.

This is why Sheila learned quickly to stomp her feet when entering the kitchen at night.She also learned to turn on the lights quickly.The stomping made the mice run away and the light made the roaches scatter.

The house always seemed dark and gloomy. The atmosphere was always on edge. There was always arguing. It became obvious this screaming was the norm for communication.

There were moments in Sheila's memory bank that no child should recall.

There was no sign of stability, emotional support or structure. She didn't experience many basic needs during her childhood.

She was left to figure things out on her own.

There were times when Sheila was beaten and her bed sheet burned her naked skin.She went to school with belt buckle marks left on her legs.
Her brother would throw his body on top of her to stop the attack. It is not uncommon for younger siblings to feel a sense of protectiveness over their older siblings. While the older sibling may be seen as more capable and independent, the younger sibling may feel a strong desire to ensure their safety and well-being.

This protective instinct can manifest in a variety of ways. For example, the younger sibling may feel the need to intervene if they perceive their older sibling to be in danger or under threat. They may also take on a more supportive role, offering emotional support or encouragement when their older sibling is facing a difficult situation.

While this dynamic was a source of strength and support. By working together and looking out for each other, siblings can build a strong bond that lasts a lifetime.

This was definitely the case for Sheila and her brother. They were inseparable. They were two people in the same exact situation. They truly created a love and connection that would follow them throughout their lives.

Sheila believed that she reminded her mother of her father. Sheila also thought that she reminded her mother of the young girl full of dreams and aspirations that she used to be. That was before her life changed and sidetracked, before Sheila's father.

That was also before the generational curses of her family took her off track.

Her mother was a workaholic. Which meant she would be with family the majority of the time. A workaholic mother is someone who has a compulsive need to work excessively and is unable to stop due to financial obligations as a single parent.

Sheila's father never paid child support.Although her

mother being a workaholic was necessary, it negatively impacted her life and relationships. Having a workaholic mother can be challenging, as she may prioritize her work over spending time with her family, leading to feelings of neglect and abandonment.

It is important to understand that workaholism is not a choice, but rather a coping mechanism for underlying emotional issues such as fear of failure.Failure was not a option for Sheila's mother. Her family had a sick thing of competition with each other.They rarely celebrated with each other.

She was determined to take care of herself and her kids. If you have a workaholic mother, try to communicate your feelings to her in a calm and non-judgmental manner. Let her know that you appreciate her hard work, but also express your need for quality time and attention. Encourage her to seek help, either through therapy or support groups, to address the underlying emotional issues that may be driving her workaholic behavior.

Remember, a workaholic mother is still a loving mother who wants the best for her family. With patience, understanding, and open communication, it is possible to overcome the challenges of having a workaholic parent and strengthen your relationship with her.

She remembers waking up in the middle of the night to the smell of smoke. These were called smoke bombs. This meant a towel would be put in a metal can and set on fire. While she and her family slept, the smoke would fill the whole house while they were sleeping. She remembers sleeping in the bed where roaches inhabited every crack and crevice of her bed.

She remembers the day her uncle (mother's brother) decided to play with all of his nieces and nephews. The game consisted of all of the girls rolling over the guys, which included their uncle and younger male cousin. Then, the uncle decided to begin taking turns kissing and touching his nieces in private places that were not approved.

How do you live in the house with your uncle and keep his secrets?

This wasn't Sheila's first time going through this because she had already been a victim of this when she was a few years younger, around 4 years old. She had been led on many trips to the store.

Trips to the store that led to the stops behind the store and her older cousin's hands inside her clothes.

She knew this wasn't right, but somehow, it was accepted.

Walking innocently through the house, doors to the restroom left wide open. Seeing uncles and her grandfather's private parts.

There were no boundaries.

How could she unsee this?

Sheila wished on a regular basis, her REAL family would show up to get her one day. She had the idea that this could not really be her reality.

How could she be born into a family and not connect with her mother or her father?

Most of the family members on her mother's side had endured incest,mental and physical abuse.

Sheila would go on later in life searching for love, acceptance and wholeness in all the wrong places and people. She was so deep into promiscuity at one point she thought Jesus himself would manifest in the room to stop her.

Sheila knew Jesus. She knew how to pray even as a child. She gave her life to Christ at an early age. She had the conviction of the Holy Spirit.But her flesh was ruling her because of her broken spirit and desire for connection.

These traumatic events in her childhood definitely would have led her to be "The Woman at the Well."

# CHAPTER 2
# You are Enough

There was something missing deep inside most of the members of Sheila's family.Theses were people who hadn't experienced being LOVED.It wasn't their fault.This is what they were born into .They were bamboozled to accept their lack thereof as truth.

Love is a complex emotion that can bring great joy and fulfillment, but for those who don't experience love, life can feel lonely and disconnected. There are many reasons why someone might not experience love, including a lack of social skills, past trauma, or simply not having met the right person yet.

For some individuals, their inability to experience love may stem from childhood experiences that have left them emotionally scarred. For example, growing up in a household where parents didn't show affection or where there was abuse can make it difficult to form healthy relationships later in life.

Others may struggle with social skills, making it difficult to form connections with others. This can be especially challenging for those with conditions such as autism or social anxiety disorder.

Regardless of the reason, it is important to remember that everyone deserves love and connection. Seeking therapy or counseling can be a helpful step in addressing underlying issues and learning new ways to form healthy relationships. Additionally, participating in activities and groups that align with personal interests can provide opportunities to meet new people and form meaningful connections.

Ultimately, while not experiencing love can be a difficult and isolating experience, it is possible to learn new skills and build relationships that bring joy and fulfillment to life.

But first you have to be able to recognize that you need LOVE and deserve LOVE.

A typical family gathering started out all fun and games until too much alcohol was in the system of most of the family members.
Liquor was the chosen method of therapy.

Sheila was judged for her beauty. She was judged for her shame. She was judged for her hardness. She was judged for her weakness. Sheila was a product of a dysfunctional family.

There were nights Sheila slept in her bed, crying and praying to the Lord to take her in her sleep. She did not want to wake up and endure another day. She asked the Lord regularly to help deal with the great stress and overwhelming feelings.

The desire for connection pushed Sheila to begin to be

promiscuous at an early age. This was one of those generational curses.

There is no handbook that lists all the generation curses of your family.However: with careful observation and prayer it can be revealed.

The physical act of sex made Sheila feel a  sense of love and acceptance. It didn't matter in that moment that it was temporary.It became her coping mechanism.Promiscuity is the act of having multiple sexual partners without commitment or attachment. This behavior is for various reasons, such as seeking physical pleasure, avoiding emotional attachment, or fulfilling a desire for intimacy.

However, promiscuous behavior does lead to emotional complications, such as guilt, shame, and loss of self-respect.Feeling desperate for love can be a tough and overwhelming experience. It's natural to want to feel loved and cared for, but it's important to remember that love can't be forced or rushed. It's important to take the time to build a healthy relationship with yourself first before seeking love from others.

In my mind, I imagine sex and any type of connection with a man  was the coping mechanism for "The Woman At The Well" . She had a deep thirst for attention and acceptance that she didn't even understand. I imagine those husbands gave her a sense of belonging. She didn't want to be alone. She had abandonment issues. After every failed relationship she immediately went to the next.

Sheila and "The Woman At The Well" had daddy-daughter issues. A father is supposed to set the standards by which a man should treat his daughter in the future. He should be the source of stability and strength.A father should be a daughter's first love.

Sheila's father was not in her life. He divorced her at 9

years old.He was supposed to be her protector and the provider.

She didn't get to see her father love, honor and cherish her mother.

Sheila needed someone in her life to tell her, "You Are Enough."

The sad news is that that wasn't expressed to her in her early years. Which gave the enemy an open door in her life.

Sheila would go on to have several failed marriages to men that didn't even qualify.

Imagine getting married not even knowing what you're supposed to feel or think about the other person to qualify for marriage. Her first husband was older than her.He had traveled and experienced life.

One day, he told her, "It is better to marry than to burn." He was trying to quote:

1 Corinthians 7:8-9

King James Version

I say, therefore, to the unmarried and widows it is good for them if they abide even as I do.
But if they cannot contain, let them marry, for it is better to marry than to burn.

Her first marriage wasn't even based on love. She married as an escape from family issues. This marriage was the most traumatic of all. During that marriage Sheila experienced rape, mental abuse, verbal abuse, emotional abuse and physical abuse.

Sheila was mentally checked out in that marriage long before it ended. Sheila had been put out of the car, left to walk home at nine months pregnant by her husband.

He had attempted to push her downstairs in order to take phone calls from women outside of the marriage.

The very touch of her husband made Sheila feel nauseous.
She no longer desired to fulfill her wifely duties.

She was very vocal about her thoughts and feelings of abuse. Sheila's husband began having sex with her while she was asleep.

There were times that she didn't even know the act had happened until she woke up with her underwear missing.She felt like she was NOTHING.

This was such a traumatic time for Sheila that she somehow blocked every time the event happened.

He was having full intercourse with her while she was in a DEEP sleep.

It is still unexplained how she remained asleep during these episodes. It was as if the Lord was shielding and protecting her from this repetitive reality.It was a state of unconsciousness.

Sheila went to the Pastor of her church and to seek help.She did not find any help or comfort.Her husband was active in ministry and even preaching in pulpit after pulpit.

Sheila also suffered a miscarriage during this marriage due to overwhelming stress in the marriage.
The day of the miscarriage Sheila went to her OBGYN due to spotting and bleeding. Within a few hours, Sheila was told to go straight to the Hospital.

She would be dropped off at the hospital by her husband to have a procedure to remove the 13-week-old infant. Her five-month-old son sat in his car seat. He told her he was going to go pay bills and he would be back to pick her up.

Sheila is 20 years old at the hospital to get the remains of the child she carried removed from her body, and her husband left her. The staff at the hospital insisted that she call someone to be with her. She could not be alone for this type of procedure. Sheila often hid the true reality of her marriage and life. She called a couple they were friends with from church.

They stayed with her and encouraged her. At 7:00pm, her husband came back to pick her up. Their friends from the church had a conversation with him.

She was only 19 years old when she married and by age 21 had endured all this after a troubled childhood. She met him in her first year of college.

When she met him, her mother had recently changed the dynamics of her life with a nervous breakdown. She was very fragile spiritually as well because her mother had opened up a dark door spiritually that led to torment in their lives.

She had shared all of this with her husband. Yet he used his spiritual knowledge, power and hidden agenda to bring more pain to her life.He became a master of spiritual abuse .

In her second marriage, Sheila went on to marry for love. She loved this man so much. She loved the color and smell of his skin. They were best friends in the beginning. They laughed often and were inseparable, like Bonnie and Clyde.

They had very similar personalities. Sheila began to feel a strong call for ministry in her life. The issue was Sheila was still figuring things out. This caused Sheila to change in many ways. While the expectations of her husband remained the same.

Distance grew in the marriage. They eventually were more like roommates. They were in separate bedrooms.

Sheila ultimately felt a deep pain and hurt due to rejection from her husband. He eventually cut off all forms of intimacy with her. There were late nights and unanswered phone calls, and then eventually, he came home in the mornings.

Sheila sacrificed to help him pursue his career desires just to be abandoned in the marriage.She often felt depressed and discouraged. Sheila was at a very low point and gained excessive weight.This wasn't a safe and healthy love. They both had behaviors that were not appropriate towards the one you love.

Sheila was forced to see the terrible things she survived were again affecting her marriage. Which led to ultimate betrayal of infidelity. Twelve years down the drain. They attempted marital counseling. Her husband verbally stated that he would not be happy if he stayed in the marriage.

He had gotten a taste of life without her before they were actually separated. There was nowhere to go from there. Sheila loved that man with every ounce of her being.That type of love was one that Sheila had to pray to God to help her release.

Sheila often asks, "Why not me," "Why can't I receive the same or greater love." She wanted to be someone's priority. Someone's only option. She began to realize she was worth being pursued. Sheila, just like I imagine the woman at the well, kept hitting love speed bumps. Letting down her walls just to be left lonely and hurt deeply.

How can any woman keep a soft heart when everything she knows says, "Be hard, protect yourself"?

I imagine Sheila and "The Woman At The Well" thinking, "When I hurt myself to keep understanding how to love you.

How do you share the greatest connections with someone yet share the same deepest hurts?
People look deeply into your eyes.They look into your very soul.Then then treat you as if you never existed.

It is a painful and confusing experience when someone you love starts to act like you don't exist. Sheila felt hurt, rejected, and even betrayed by this behavior. However, those actions were not a reflection of her or value as a person.

John 4:16-18

16 He told her, "Go, call your husband and come back."17 "I have no husband," she replied. Jesus said to her, "You are right when you say you have no husband. 18 The fact is, you have had five husbands, and the man you now have is not your husband. What you have just said is quite true."

The Woman At The Well had a addition.Her drug of choice was MEN.
Addiction can be a complex issue, and one of the underlying factors that can contribute to addiction is a lack of love or connection in one's life. When someone feels unloved or disconnected from others, they may turn to drugs, alcohol, or other addictive behaviors as a way to cope with these difficult emotions.

Studies have shown that people who have experienced trauma or neglect in childhood are more likely to struggle with addiction later in life. This is because early experiences can shape the way our brains develop, and if we don't receive the love and support we need during this critical period, it can leave us more vulnerable to addiction.

It's important to a person's history in order to fully understand a person's actions and way of thinking.

Addictions and low self-esteem issues can be traced back to lack of basic needs not being met in early development.
Addictions are forms of coping mechanisms.
Truth is The Lord loves us. There is nothing or anyone that can separate us from the love of God.

In the word of God, the Lord continually says:

"You are Enough"

Romans 5:7-9

7 For scarcely for a righteous man will one die: yet peradventure for a good man some would even dare to die.8 But God commendeth his love toward us, in that, while we were yet sinners, Christ died for us.9 Much more then, being now justified by his blood, we shall be saved from wrath through him.

Psalm 34:4-8-4 I sought the Lord, and he answered me; he delivered me from all my fears. 5 Those who look at him are radiant; their faces are never covered with shame. 6 This poor man called, and the Lord heard him; he saved him out of all his troubles. 7 The angel of the Lord encamps around those who fear him, and he delivers them. 8 Taste and see that the Lord is good;

blessed is the one who takes refuge in him.

John 14:27 Peace I leave with you; my peace I give you. I do not give to you as the world gives. Do not let your hearts be troubled, and do not be afraid. Psalm 23:4 Even though I walk through the darkest valley, I will fear no evil, for you are with me; your rod and your staff, they comfort me

Psalm 139:14

14 I praise you because I am fearfully and wonderfully made; your works are wonderful, I know that fully well.

Imagine how different the lives of Sheila and the woman at the wells could have been if someone had just said,

# "You are Enough."

**Lyrics – You Are Enough by Elevation Worship**

**My highest joy**
**Love of my heart**
**You are**
**All that's good**
**Flows from Your mercy**
**To us**
**Here's my heart**
**Make it Yours**
**And I will sing**

If I lose it all
You're enough
If I gain the world
You're enough
My joy is complete
Jesus, You are enough for me
Empty we came
For You gave Your grace
To us
And when riches fade
Still You remain Our God
Here's my heart
Make it Yours
And I will sing
If I lose it all
You're enough
If I gain the world
You're enough
My joy is complete
Jesus, You are enough for me
You can take my life
And all I have
I will sing Your worth
With all I am
You can take my life
And all I have
I will sing Your worth
The hope I've found
If I lose it all
You're enough
If I gain the world

You're enough
My joy is complete
Jesus You are enough for me
Jesus You are enough for me
Jesus You are enough for me
You're all I need
You're everything
Jesus You are enough for me
You're all I need
You're everything
Jesus You are enough for me
You're all I need
You're everything
Jesus You are enough for me
You're all I need
You're everything
Jesus You are enough for me
You're all I need
You're everything
Jesus You are enough for me

Source: Musixmatch
Songwriters: Wade Joye / Mack Donald Iii Brock /
Christopher Joel Brown / London Weidberg Gatch
You Are Enough lyrics © Be Essential Son

# CHAPTER 3
## Brokenness

Psalms 147:3

Psalms 147:3 in Other Translations

3 He healeth the broken in heart, and bindeth up their wounds. 3 He heals the brokenhearted and binds up their wounds. 3 He heals the brokenhearted and bandages their wounds.

The meaning of brokenness is a condition in which something is badly damaged and unable to continue or work correctly.

How do you know when you're broken?

Signs of a broken woman include, but are not limited to:

Low self-esteem.

Fear of abandonment.

Lack of confidence.
Insecurities.

Looking at kind gestures with skepticism.

Inability to show affection.

Feelings   of   worthlessness   following   a   failed

relationship.

Promiscuity.

When a woman is Broken it doesn't matter what type of relationships she tries to have. They will all fail.

Sheila and the woman at the well would need to address the brokenness from the inside out in order to be whole. Brokenness for Sheila started with the break in her relationship with her father.

Sheila didn't have enough memories with her father. A good memory was he used to let her roller-skate inside the house. Sheila felt loved by her father when he was present.

After her parents separated her father would come and visit. He would also take her and her brother on outings. Sometimes they would spend the night with him at her grandfather's house.
One day Sheila's dad picked her and her brother up to go to the movies. On the way to the movies they stopped at a strange house. She was looking in the doorway of this house and there stood a little girl. The little girl looked just like Sheila. This was creepy. She was trying to figure out who this little girl was.

Her father came out of the house with the little girl and then another little girl. Her dad then says, "This is your sister".
That was the introduction.

Introducing a child to a new sibling can be an exciting and sometimes overwhelming experience for both the child and the parent. Sheila's dad clearly had no clue.There was no preparation,Sheila didn't have any insight.

He was married to her mom and he's introducing her and her brother to a new sibling. She also happens to look just like Sheila and is about her same age.
That was very awkward. Sheila was only around 8 years old.

How was she going to tell her mom about this?

Did her mom already know about this? So many thoughts raced through her mind.

How did her daddy process this news or the process of delivery was appropriate.

This further contributed to Sheila's brokenness.

Brokenness will keep you in cycles.It will keep you in relationships longer than you should have stayed.It will make you accept the bare minimum.

Truth is you deserved the world.

Can you imagine being so mentally traumatized you fall for men based on the type of father he was to his kids. Or at least the type of father he led Sheila to believe he was. She admired them because they actually accepted the role of being a father.

Sheila found herself smitten in the way men talked about their kids.
Especially if a man had a daughter.

There was still a broken little girl inside of her that wanted to be loved. She wanted a dad to feel loved in that way.

Sheila's life was full of brokenness. Most of the people in Sheila's entire life had betrayed her trust, used her and / or abused her.She was needed for things .

Noone actually really saw her.

How was this possible?

She allowed everyone to dump on her. She hated her heart.

Why did she love so hard?

Why was she so trusting?

Why did she have to be so forgiving?

She couldn't say "no'". Sheila had experienced so much in her life her empathy for others put her in critical condition.

She didn't set boundaries with others. I think she was afraid of rejection if she did.

The final straw for Sheila was a series of events.

# CHAPTER 4
# **Desperation**

James 4:8
New International Version

8 Come near to God, and he will come near to you. Wash your hands, you sinners, and purify your hearts, you double-minded.

Sheila found herself with several failed marriages.Multiple failed relationships can be a tough and emotionally draining experience for women. It is normal for women to feel a range of emotions after such experiences, including sadness, disappointment, anger, frustration, and even self-doubt.

After going through multiple failed relationships, some women may feel like they are not good enough or that they will never find the right partner.

However, it is important to remember that failed relationships are not a reflection of one's worth or ability to love.

It is essential to take time to heal and reflect on past relationships before diving into a new one. This can help women gain a better understanding of their own needs and desires in a relationship and help them make more informed choices in the future.

Ultimately, it is important for women to remember that they deserve to be with someone who values and respects them, and it may take time to find the right person.

With patience, self-care, and a positive outlook, women can move forward and find happiness in their personal lives.

Sheila becomes a professional at ghosting people in her relationships. Ghosting in a relationship is when one person suddenly stops responding to the other person's messages and calls, seemingly disappearing without any explanation or closure. This can be a frustrating and hurtful experience for the person who has been ghosted.

There are many reasons why someone might choose to ghost in a relationship. Sometimes, people may not feel ready or willing to have a difficult conversation with their partner about why they want to end the relationship. Other times, they may feel overwhelmed or stressed out and decide to withdraw from the relationship without communicating this to their partner. Additionally, some people may choose to ghost as a way to avoid confrontation or conflict.

Regardless of the reason, being ghosted can be a painful experience for the other person. It's important to remember that everyone deserves clear communication and closure in a relationship. If you feel like you are being ghosted, it may be helpful to reach out to your partner and try to have an open and honest conversation about what is going on. If they are not willing to communicate, it may be time to move on and find someone who is willing to give you the respect and communication that you deserve.

She wanted love but ran when it felt close. She had famous scripted text messages and emails to ghost people. When feelings got involved, she reverted back to being a little girl who couldn't communicate her thoughts and feelings without fear.
When "The Woman At The Well" had her encounter with Jesus, she was living with a man that was not her husband.

She had clearly reached a point of desperation to accept this.
Sheila had wasted over five years in a dysfunctional situationship with a man who was not her husband.

Sounds familiar huh?

Just like "The Woman At The Well".

That relationship was toxic and sent straight from hell.

Like so many women who have surrendered their lives to Christ. But get tired and desperate in the wait. They find themselves trying to help God with his plans. They find themselves settling as a second choice or side option. They decide to settle and believe the lie that a man is better than no man.

That entanglement became a spiritual stronghold. Sheila thought at one point that she truly loved this man. The enemy is very cleaver.He knows what our flesh desires.They had formed a trauma bond and soul tie based on molestations from both of their childhoods.They felt a sick sense of obligation and acceptance to each other.

Unlike other people they each had been involved intimately with.
They created a safe space for each other that was blinded to all the toxicity of reality.

One night, Sheila sat in her bed praying in the Spirit for deliverance from this stronghold when suddenly he was knocking on her front door.It was though Satan sent him to stop her prayers.

He hurt Sheila on every level. Sheila once woke up in the morning from a dream about him with tears flowing down her face.
Even in her dreams, he made her cry.

She could almost calculate when he would show up.
During the course of the situationship with this man Sheila would not move forward with men that could have been God sent.

The enemy used this man to keep Sheila under some sick form of mind control. He even got married while dating Sheila.
He said he was just co-parenting, yet ended in marriage to the mother of his son.

Lies he told her regularly:

-He married just for his son.

-He married for a place to live.
-He was getting a divorce.
-They will live happily ever after.

She was so bound by that stronghold that it turned into years off and on.
She knew he was lying to her.
But she was broken and wanted to be loved badly. She had convinced herself one day they would be together.

Then, the day came that her eyes were opened. She realized she would never trust him. He was a liar and a deceiver.She had been pressing into the Lord for wisdom and discernment.

After much prayer and self-control, The Lord broke that stronghold in her life.

Praise be to the Lord.

James 4:7 Submit yourselves, then, to God. Resist the devil ...
Be subject therefore unto God; but resist the devil, and he will flee from you. ...

Submit therefore to God and stand against Satan, and he will flee from you.

We must be desperate for the presence and will of God. Desperation to ask for forgiveness and truly be ready to surrender. Her past sin and choices had disgusted her. Sheila was tired of herself. I can imagine the woman at the well felt the same.

I imagine her friends labeled her as the talk of town. Just

THE WOMAN AT THE WELL

like the labels of the Woman at the well. Everyone wants to listen to the drama, but they are not willing to pray and encourage.

She wanted to focus on God's grace, his peace and feel his forgiveness. She desired a true relationship with Christ.

2 Corinthians 4:18

18 So we fix our eyes not on what is seen, but on what is unseen since what is seen is temporary, but what is unseen is eternal.
True desperation brings you to a point of whatever it takes Lord.

Here I am Lord.

1 Peter 5:7,

ESV

Casting all your anxieties on him because he cares for you. 1 All to Jesus I surrender; All to him I freely give; I will ever love and trust him, In his presence daily life.
Refrain: I surrender all, I surrender all, all to thee, my blessed Savior, I surrender all.

Romans 8:35-39

35 Who shall separate us from the love of Christ? Shall trouble or hardship or persecution or famine or nakedness or danger or sword? 36 As it is written: "For your sake, we face death all day long; we are considered as sheep to be slaughtered."[a]37 No, in all these things, we are more than conquerors through him who loved

us. 38 For I am convinced that neither death nor life, neither angels nor demons,[b] neither the present nor the future, nor any powers, 39 neither height nor depth nor anything else in all creation, will be able to separate us from the love of God that is in Christ Jesus our Lord.

# CHAPTER 5
# When "I AM" is on the Scene

"I AM" is the most powerful command statement there is. It means that God is whatever and whoever we need him to be.

It's the power of God being spoken to you for comfort and reassurance that all our needs are already met.

Ultimately, the presence of "I AM" in our lives is what and who we were Thirsty for from the beginning.

I am the Bread of Life (John 6:35)

I am the Light of the World (John 8:12)

I am the Door (John 10:9)

I am the Good Shepherd (John 10:11,14)

I am the Resurrection and the Life (John 11:25)

I am the Way and the Truth and the Life (John 14:6)

I am the Vine (John 15:1,5)

When "I AM" shows up on the scene, healing and restoration take place. Lives are changed. Transformation takes place.

Romans 12

New International Version

A Living Sacrifice

12 Therefore, I urge you, brothers and sisters, in view of God's mercy, to offer your bodies as a living sacrifice, holy and pleasing to God—this is your true and proper worship. 2 Do not conform to the pattern of this world, but be transformed by the renewing of your mind. Then you will be able to test and approve what God's will be— his good, pleasing and perfect will.

Sheila eventually surrendered her will to the will of Christ. She began to experience the life Christ intended for her. A life of self-love and love for others. She went on a journey of healing and forgiveness. She created boundaries in relationships. The Lord gave her an internal peace. It cost her several relationships. But her relationship with Christ was worth it all.

You can't have a true experience with "I AM" and remain the same.
When Jesus spoke to the woman at the well, her whole life also changed.

One encounter with Jesus
Christ changed everything. Even in your situation now. It only takes one touch. One word from "I AM".

It didn't matter that she was a Samaritan woman. It didn't matter that she went to get water at an awkward time of day to avoid people.

When Sheila had a real encounter with "I AM," it didn't matter how many mistakes she had made.

The failed marriages didn't matter. "I AM" revealed he was always on the scene. He knew "the rest of the story."

He met her right where she was to give her eternal life. It was never about the physical water. It was always about the "living water."

John 4:13

Jesus answered, "Everyone who drinks this water will be thirsty again, 14 but whoever drinks the water I give them will never thirst. Indeed, the water I give them will become in them a spring of water welling up to eternal life."

He did not see her sin. He only mentioned her life to reveal that he was "I AM."

Colossians 1:22

But now he has reconciled you by his physical body through death, to present you before God as a people who are holy, faultless, and without blame.

Exodus 15:2

"The LORD is my strength and my defense; he has become my salvation. He is my God, and I will praise him, my father's God, and I will exalt him.

2 Samuel 22:3

My God is my rock, in whom I take refuge, my shield and the horn of my salvation. He is my stronghold, my refuge and my savior— from violent people, you save me.

John 4:23
Yet a time is coming and has now come when the true worshipers will worship the Father in the Spirit and in truth, for they are the kind of worshipers the Father seeks. 24 God is spirit, and his worshipers must worship in the Spirit and in truth."

25 The woman said, "I know that Messiah (called Christ) "is coming. When he comes, he will explain everything to us."
Then Jesus declared, "I, the one speaking to you—I am he."
Please share your testimony with others. The world needs more transparent Christians to share the Power, the Word and saving grace of Jesus Christ.
Blessings

# ABOUT THE AUTHOR

My name is Stephanie Seaton. I was born the oldest child of my parents.My father was the oldest child of 7 children. He grew up in an abusive family. He witnessed domestic violence against his mother at the hands of his father. As a young man, he grew brave and decided to stand in protection of his mother. That had a terrible price attached to it. He began to be the main victim of physical, mental and emotional abuse.

My mother grew up in a family with similar yet more abusive tendencies. My parents dated briefly. They were drawn together by the trauma. After my conception, they were married.

A Lot of my childhood is a blur. I'm sure there were some bright sky rainbow moments. However, long sad days seem to be more prevalent.

My parents separated and later divorced. My father eventually moved to California. The divorce and move was literally between my dad, my mom and my sister and I. These were two broken people that gave it the best shot they knew.

I truly believe the Holy Spirit led and guided me during my entire life, even before I asked him into my heart. There is no other explanation because I am still in my right mind able to write this book.

I was a very quiet child. I played alone a lot. I had quite a vivid imagination, actually. I even had my own imaginary world many times in my life. In the imaginary world, I could have a voice and have imaginary friendships because I felt so lonely.

I remember dreaming lots of special dreams of the bible, seeing myself teaching and or preaching. I had one dream over and over of a spirit like a genie taking over all my relatives inside my grandparents' house. I was on the outside looking in the back window of the house. I knew at an early age that the Lord was in my life. I just didn't know the full weight of that.

I remember at the age of nine years old feeling compelled to get up and go to the altar to surrender my life to Christi didn't even consciously know I was getting up.

My middle school years were very challenging for me. I had absent parents. I experienced peer pressure, dysfunctions at home, and basically felt lost.

I had a lot to deal with. In middle school, I attempted suicide as a cry for help.Then came high school. High school was when I began dealing with depression.

My mother and I had a very conflicting relationship. I've had lots of therapy throughout the years. I also had several women in my life that nurtured me and guided me in different stages of lifes.

I went to a Shambach church revival, where I was introduced to the filling of the Holy Spirit. By the time

I graduated from High School at 17 years old , I had become a mother to my mom, my sister and myself.

By age 17, I had also endured forms of molestation by two family members. One on my mom's side of the family. The other on my dad's side of the family.

Both of which were never held accountable.

I do not look like what I've been through. I have had multiple failed marriages that I was not equipped for.

I have two amazing sons. I call them "my heartbeats".

My oldest son, Christian was a "Saving Grace" at one of the lowest periods in my life. He said Mom "We need you to get it together".

I have found that same "Saving Grace"in the eyes of my youngest son Isaiah's eyes every day.

They are my Reason.

I thank God,he found favor in me to be called mom.

As an adult woman, I have fought hard through prayer, counseling and tears to be the best woman I can be. It has not been easy.My life has been a life of steady bumps, drops, turns and yet VICTORY.

I committed my life to ministry back in 2013.I was active serving in various areas until 2015.I resigned from ministry.

I resigned due to the heaviness of the call. I vowed not to go back into ministry unless the Lord sent someone to get me.I hid in the background.

After 7 years,he did just that.He send people in my church to get me connected into the ministry.I had been attending church for over a year.I was going and rushing to leave.Then the Holy Spirit arrested me.I eventually ended up prostrate on my bedroom floor .I had to surrender to the call I had been running from .

My prayer is that everyone who reads this book sees Jesus Christ. These were some very dark and heavy times in my life. But The Lord was with me and kept me in ALL stages.Even when I was angry at him.

He loved and provided for me MOST.

I remember asking the Lord," Why did he allow all these things to happen to me."

His reply was, "It was all for ministry".

In 2015, I would later go on to start a non-profit women's ministry group (Diamonds in the Rough) for broken women. The Lord had prepared me all my life for the call.

**To God be all the Glory!**
**I'm Thankful for it all!**

Made in the USA
Middletown, DE
15 October 2023

40725544R00038